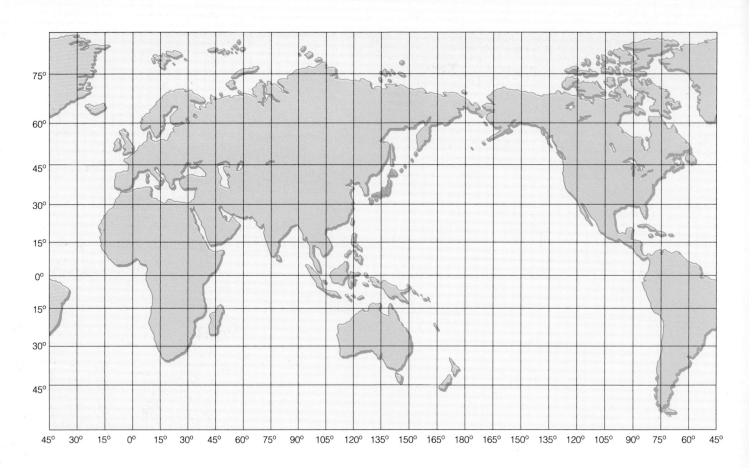

JAPAN

John Baines

MACDONALD YOUNG BOOKS

First published in 1994 by Simon & Schuster Young Books
© Simon & Schuster Young Books 1994. Reprinted in 1996
and 1997 by Macdonald Young Books.

Published in paperback in Great Britain in 1997 and 1998
by Macdonald Young Books.

Macdonald Young Books, an imprint of Wayland publishers Ltd
61 Western Road
Hove
East Sussex
BN3 1JD

Find Macdonald Young Books on the internet at http://www.myb.co.uk

Design	Roger Kohn
Editor	Diana Russell
DTP editor	Helen Swansbourne
Picture research	Valerie Mulcahy
Illustration	Malcolm Porter
	János Márffy
Consultant	David Barrs
Commissioning Editor	Debbie Fox

We are grateful fo the following for permission
to reproduce photographs:
Front Cover: Peter Rauter/TRIP, *below,* Robert Harding Picture
Library, *above;* Camera Press, pages 19 (JUng Kwan Chi), 35
below (Peter Abbey/LNS); J Allan Cash, pages 18 *above,* 20,
21,29, 30; Colorific!, pages 17 (Mike Yamashita), 33 (Eiji
Miyazawa/Black Star); Eye Ubitquitous/TRIP, pages 27 *inset*
and 28 (Frank Leather), 35 *above* (Paul Thompson);
Greenpeace, page 39 (Morgan); Robert Harding Picture
Library, pages 25, 26,27 *below;* The Image Bank, pages 36
below (JulesZalon), 38 (G Colliva); Japan National Tourist
Organization, page 13; Magnum, pages 18 *below* (Ian Berry),
22 (Bruno Barbey), 36 *above* (Paul Fusco); Nissan Mortor
Manuafacturing (UK) Ltd, pages 31, 32; Orion Press, pages 8,
9, 12, 37; Peter Rauter/TRIP, page 42; Rex Features/Sipa-
Press, page 24 (Toyosaki); Tony Stone Worldwide, pages 15
(Thierry Cazabon), 16 (Matthew Harris), 23 *below,* 27 *above,*
40; Taisei Corporation, page 41; Telegraph Colour Library,
pages 11 (VCL) 23 *above;* Toyota AG, page 43; Yamaha-
Kemble Music (UK) Ltd, page 24; Yamaha Motor Europe, page
34 *below;* Zefa, page 14 (Goebel).

The statistics give in this book are the most up to date
available at the time of going to press

Printed in Hong Kong by Wing King Tong Co Ltd

A CIP catalogue record for this book is available from the British Library

ISBN: 0 7500 2450 X

C
O
N
T
E
N
T
S

Words that are explained in the glossary are printed in
SMALL CAPITALS the first time they are mentioned in the text.
Charts and diagrams include statistics for the former USSR.

● INTRODUCTION

The Japanese word for Japan 'Nippon' means source of the sun, from which comes a popular western nickname for Japan: land of the rising sun. Today we are more likely to think of Japan as the home of the Sony Walkman, the Suzuki motorbike, the Pentax camera and countless makes of car. All these things play a very important part in our lives and in the economies of all western countries. But these are really very recent developments.

Japan is an old country with ancient traditions. These are very different from those of other countries because Japan remained isolated from outside influences until after 1854. The traditions remain, although the Japanese way of life has changed dramatically.

Japan is now a highly successful industrial nation and shares many similarities with other major industrial countries: large, crowded cities with congested streets, high-rise buildings,

▼ *The ritual of the Tea Ceremony or* cha-no-yu *is 600 years old. It is held in a simple room. By concentrating on the tea making the participants aim to achieve a feeling of peacefulness.*

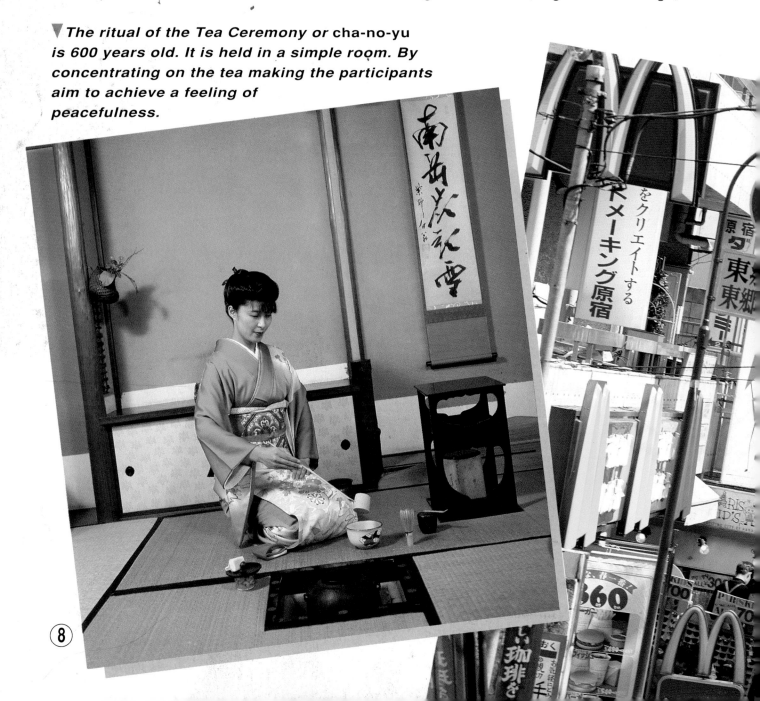

shops, offices and factories. The people are well off and live in comfortable homes. Their health care and education systems are good. But there are environmental problems like those in other developed countries: loss of countryside, traffic congestion, air pollution and water pollution.

This book is an introduction to Japan. You will find information about the country and its people, the climate and the natural resources, how the Japanese earn their livings and spend their leisure time. The Japanese economic success story is something we cannot afford to ignore.

JAPAN AT A GLANCE

- Area: 377,781 square kilometres
- Population (1990): 123,460,000
- Density: about 320 people per square kilometre
- Capital: Tokyo, population 8.3 million
- Other main cities: Yokohama 3.1 million; Osaka 2.6 million; Nagoya 2.1 million; Sapporo 1.6 million; Kyoto 1.4 million
- Highest mountain: Mount Fuji, 3776 metres
- Language: Japanese
- Main religions: Shintoism, Buddhism, Christianity
- Currency: YEN, written as ¥
- Economy: Highly industrialised
- Major natural resources: Fish, timber, fast flowing rivers
- Major products: Automobiles, electrical and electronic goods, textiles, steel, machines and robots, rice
- Environment: Severe pollution of air, water and land near industrial areas, but controls are now much stricter

◀ *The crowded streets of Tokyo are similar to any big modern city.*

THE LANDSCAPE

Japan is a country made up of islands. There are four large ones, Hokkaido, Honshu, Shikoku and Kyushu, and about 3000 much smaller ones. The islands run north to south for over 2500 kilometres. To the west about 500 kilometres across the Sea of Japan is the mainland of Asia. To the east the nearest countries are Canada and the USA about 7000 kilometres away across the Pacific Ocean.

Mountains cover more than three-quarters of Japan. Fast flowing rivers have cut steep narrow valleys into their sides and there are many beautiful lakes along the valleys. The east coast is craggy and has many inlets in contrast to the west coast which has long sweeping shores. There is little flat land. Only 15 per cent of Japan is level enough for farming and building. Small plains occur around the coast. The Kanto Plain is one of the largest. It is where Tokyo, the capital of Japan, is located.

Volcanoes are found all over Japan. Although many are extinct geologists believe 67 are still active. The most famous is Mount Fuji which, at 3776 metres, is Japan's highest mountain.

Every year Japan has hundreds of earthquakes. Many are

▶ **Japan is a very mountainous and beautiful country, with varied scenery. The mountains of the interior contrast with a coastline of cliffs, inlets and sweeping bays.**

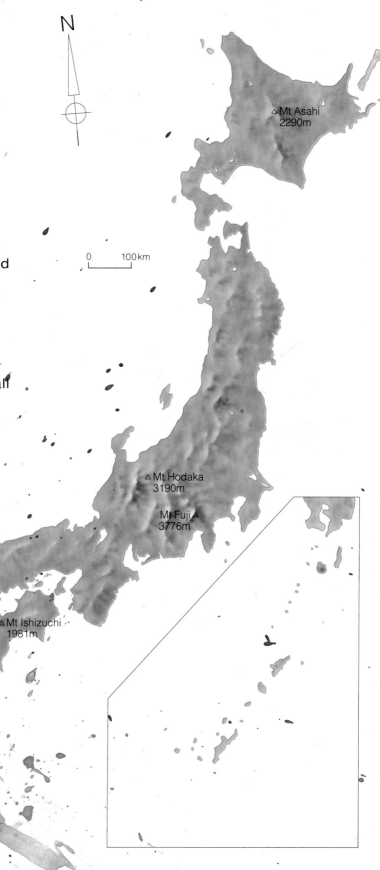

N

0   100km

△Mt Asahi
2290m

△Mt Hodaka
3190m

Mt Fuji △
3776m

△Mt Ishizuchi
1981m

△Mt Kuju
1787m

◀ *Of all the Shinto religious sites, Mount Fuji is the most sacred because of its beauty and size.*

KEY FACTS

● Japan is roughly one and a half times the size of Britain.

● No part of Japan is more than 121 kilometres from the sea.

● Japan has about 20,000 hot springs.

● Japan has 67 active volcanoes; geologists watch 17 constantly in case they show signs of erupting.

● Mount Fuji last erupted in 1707.

● Japan has four earthquakes a day, but few are even felt.

very small, but it is quite common for buildings to sway and ornaments to fall off shelves. However, this has not stopped the Japanese building skyscrapers. They are designed to sway gently as the ground moves so they do not collapse. Occasionally there are strong earthquakes, which cause terrible damage. Tokyo was destroyed by one in 1923. The city caught fire and 143,000 people died. This earthquake also caused a tidal wave 10 metres high which swept inland causing more death and destruction.

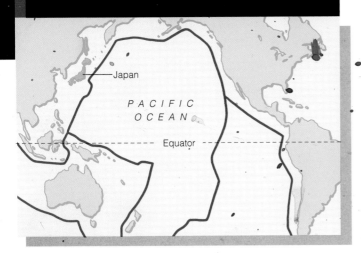

Japan

PACIFIC OCEAN

Equator

◀ *The Earth's crust consists of several plates. Around the Pacific earthquakes and volcanic activity occur where plates meet. This area is known as the Pacific Ring, here marked in red.*

● CLIMATE AND WEATHER

Japan lies between latitudes 24°N and 45°N. The difference is the same as between southern England and southern Egypt or between Montreal and the Gulf of Mexico. In the north the summers are short, cool and damp and the winters long and cold with snow lying on the ground for up to four months a year. In the south temperatures are about 15°C higher throughout the year. At Sapporo on Hokkaido the temperature ranges between -6°C and 20°C; at Okinawa in the south the range is 10°C to 32°C.

Seasonal winds called monsoons cause differences in the climate between west and east coasts. Cold winter winds from the mainland of Asia bring rain and snow to the west coast. Niigata has 194 millimetres of rain and snow in January. The east coast is still cold and windy but is much drier and brighter. Tokyo only averages 48 millimetres of rain and snow each winter.

In summer warm, moist winds blow across Japan from the Pacific Ocean. They are very humid and with the summer heat, the weather can be very uncomfortable.

Ocean currents also influence the climate. A branch of the warm Kuroshio current from the tropics passes along the shores of western Japan. It warms the cold air blowing from the mainland in winter. Warm air absorbs more moisture than cold air and this increases winter rainfall on the west coast. The cold Oyashio current from the Arctic runs along the east of Hokkaido and where it meets the warm current there are bad fogs.

The seasons are very important to the Japanese, especially spring and the flowering of the cherry trees. Newspapers report where and when the trees are at their best.

▼ *Typhoons regularly hit Japan, mainly between July and November. They start over the south-west Pacific as small areas of low pressure. By the time they reach Japan the very strong winds spiral upwards and cause much damage.*

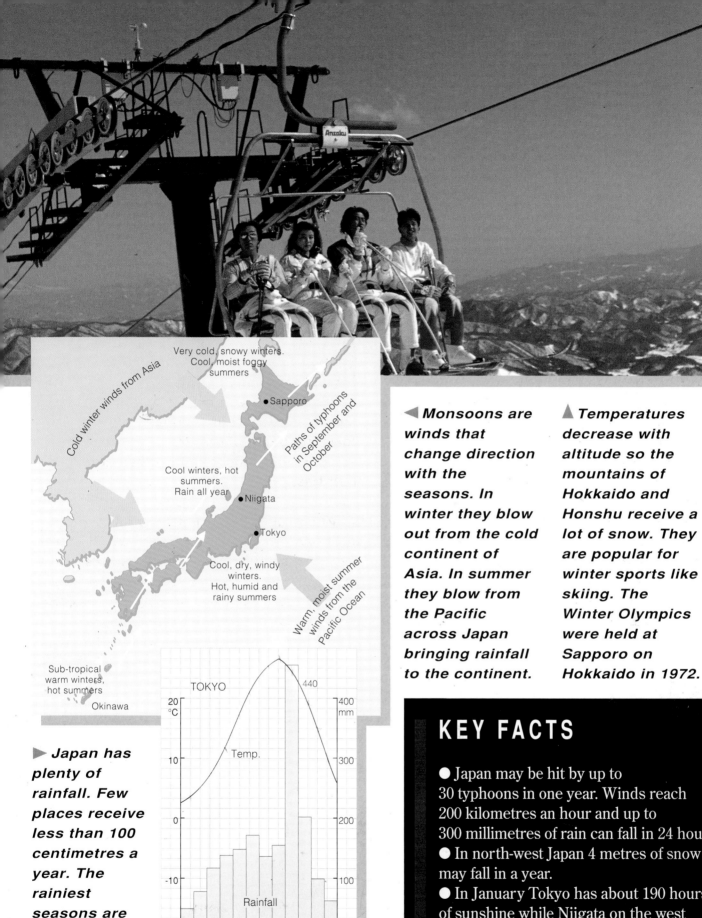

Very cold, snowy winters. Cool, moist foggy summers

Cold winter winds from Asia

● Sapporo

Paths of typhoons in September and October

Cool winters, hot summers. Rain all year

● Niigata

● Tokyo

Cool, dry, windy winters. Hot, humid and rainy summers

Warm, moist summer winds from the Pacific Ocean

Sub-tropical warm winters, hot summers

Okinawa

◀ **Monsoons are winds that change direction with the seasons. In winter they blow out from the cold continent of Asia. In summer they blow from the Pacific across Japan bringing rainfall to the continent.**

▲ **Temperatures decrease with altitude so the mountains of Hokkaido and Honshu receive a lot of snow. They are popular for winter sports like skiing. The Winter Olympics were held at Sapporo on Hokkaido in 1972.**

TOKYO

20 °C

440

400 mm

Temp.

10

300

0

200

Rainfall

-10

100

J F M A M J J A S O N D

▶ **Japan has plenty of rainfall. Few places receive less than 100 centimetres a year. The rainiest seasons are spring and autumn.**

KEY FACTS

● Japan may be hit by up to 30 typhoons in one year. Winds reach 200 kilometres an hour and up to 300 millimetres of rain can fall in 24 hours.
● In north-west Japan 4 metres of snow may fall in a year.
● In January Tokyo has about 190 hours of sunshine while Niigata on the west coast barely 255 kilometres away gets only about 56 hours.

NATURAL RESOURCES

Japan is an economic superpower like the USA. The USA and Japan are the world's main industrial countries. Unlike the USA, Japanese industry does not have the advantage of large local supplies of fossil fuels or raw materials. Fossil fuels, such as coal and oil, provide energy to produce metals from raw materials, like iron ore, and to drive machines that make products like motor cars and TV sets.

Japan has very little coal. There are mines on the islands of Hokkaido and Kyushu but the coal is poor quality and expensive to mine. Small deposits of oil occur under the land and the sea in northern Japan. However, most coal and oil are imported.

Japan's energy comes mainly from oil (57 per cent) and coal (18 per cent). Coal and oil are used to generate about half of the country's electricity. Water power (hydro-electricity) and nuclear power generate the rest. Japan is developing nuclear power stations to avoid relying on imported fossil fuels (coal and oil). In 1991 there were 39 working nuclear power stations, 11 being built and three planned.

▲ *The Chiba iron and steel plant. Plants like this use huge quantities of natural resources.*

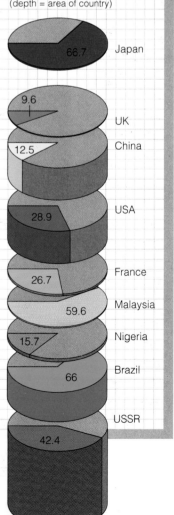

% OF LAND WOODED AND FORESTED, 1990
(depth = area of country)

- 66.7 Japan
- 9.6 UK
- 12.5 China
- 28.9 USA
- 26.7 France
- 59.6 Malaysia
- 15.7 Nigeria
- 66 Brazil
- 42.4 USSR

KEY FACTS

● 67% of Japan is covered with forest. It is the tenth most forested country in the world.
● Japan mines 96,000 tonnes of iron ore a year but uses 124 million tonnes.
● Japan produces 1% of the oil and 11% of the natural gas it uses.
● Japan imports raw materials like iron ore and exports manufactured products like cars and electrical goods.

These power stations need only a few kilos of uranium fuel instead of thousands of tonnes of oil or coal.

Japan produces few of the raw materials it needs. It mines small quantities of iron ore, copper, zinc, lead, gold and silver. Although it produces very few raw materials, Japan is the world's second largest consumer of tin and the third largest consumer of iron ore, oil and rubber.

Japan is one of the most forested countries of the world but it still has to import timber. Some comes from the

▲ *The Kurobe dam in the North Alps makes hydro-electricity using the energy of falling water. With steep sided valleys, fast flowing streams and plentiful rainfall Japan can produce a quarter of its electricity like this.*

tropical rainforests in nearby countries like Malaysia and Indonesia. Environmentalists are worried that logging is destroying these forests, the wildlife and the ways of life of people who live there. Timber is also imported from North America.

POPULATION

Almost everyone in Japan has similar physical characteristics. This is because most people are descended from the immigrants who came from the mainland of Asia and settled in the south-west of Japan. In general the Japanese have straight black hair, a medium-coloured skin, dark brown or black eyes and very little hair on their faces or bodies.

Because Japan is so mountainous most people settled on the small plains around the coast. They gathered in villages and small towns, making their living from farming and fishing.

Over the last 100 years the population has grown from around 40 million to 123 million but about 90 per cent of the people still live on the coastal plains. The plains between Tokyo and Kyushu are among the most densely populated areas in the world with around 14,000 people to every square kilometre.

Japanese homes are quite small. The home of a middle-class family of four only

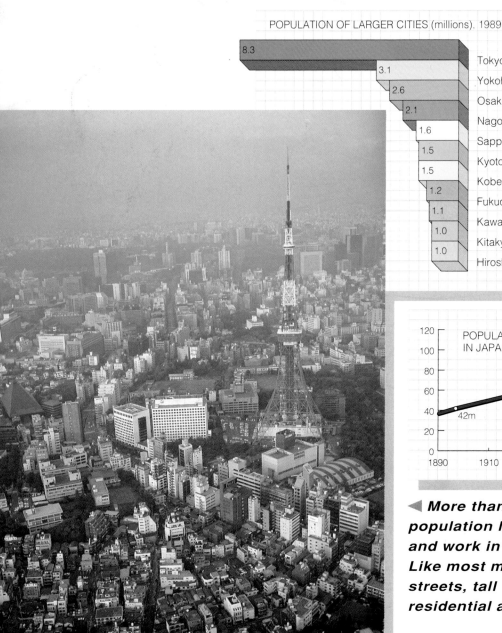

POPULATION OF LARGER CITIES (millions), 1989

8.3	Tokyo
3.1	Yokohama
2.6	Osaka
2.1	Nagoya
1.6	Sapporo
1.5	Kyoto
1.5	Kobe
1.2	Fukuoka
1.1	Kawasaki
1.0	Kitakyushu
1.0	Hiroshima

◀ *Japan has 11 cities of over 1 million people. With the exception of Sapporo they are all in the south.*

▼ *Between 1870 and 1970 the population grew from 30 to 100 million. Now the increase is much less, only 0.3 per cent a year.*

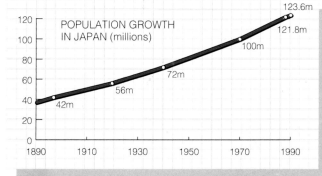

POPULATION GROWTH IN JAPAN (millions)

42m · 56m · 72m · 100m · 121.8m · 123.6m

◀ *More than three-quarters of the population live in large cities like Tokyo and work in factories, shops and offices. Like most modern cities, Tokyo has busy streets, tall office blocks and large residential areas.*

has two or three rooms, plus kitchen, bathroom and toilet. The most common Japanese-style room is fitted with tatami mats made from tightly matted rice stalks. A large cupboard stores bedding. In the centre of the room is a low table around which people sit. At night the table is moved aside, and the bedding laid out on a futon on the floor. Most Japanese homes now have at least one western-style room, usually the kitchen which will often have a table and chairs like those in western kitchens.

KEY FACTS

● Japan is the seventh most populous country in the world.
● 99.2% of the population is Japanese, 0.6% Korean and 0.2% Chinese and other nationalities.
● Tokyo, and the area around it, houses 30 million people, making it one of the largest metropolises in the world.
● There are almost 40 million homes in Japan.
● 99.4% of Japanese homes have colour TV sets.

▲ *Japanese homes are small. Rooms are designed so that different activities can take place at different times. They are simply decorated and furnished to allow this. Internal walls are thin and can slide back to create larger spaces.*

◀ Away from the cities some old villages and towns remain. Although over 70 per cent of Japanese live in towns and cities, they still feel a strong attachment to the countryside.

▼ An old Ainu man, a descendant of one of the original inhabitants of Japan.

THE AINU

When the first immigrants arrived from the Asian mainland they found the islands of Japan already inhabited by a people known as the Ainu. Today there are only about 24,000 Ainu left and they live mainly on the island of Hokkaido. They have their own language and cultural traditions but, like minority groups in many parts of the world, feel neglected by the government.

DAILY LIFE

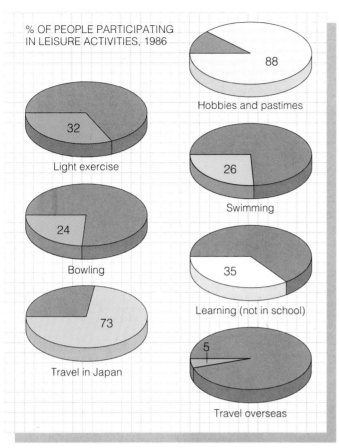

% OF PEOPLE PARTICIPATING
IN LEISURE ACTIVITIES, 1986

32
Light exercise

24
Bowling

73
Travel in Japan

88
Hobbies and pastimes

26
Swimming

35
Learning (not in school)

5
Travel overseas

▲ *The popularity of different leisure activities.*

▶*At school all children wear uniform, study the same syllabus, the same textbooks and take the same examinations. There is little time for them to develop individual personalities. Many parents now feel the system makes their children unhappy.*

Western visitors to Japan often feel that the people are very different from themselves. The Japanese have a very ancient culture which, despite the influence of western ideas, especially over the past 40 years, remains very strong.

Compared to people in western countries, the Japanese seem to enjoy the friendship of groups. They often work, relax and worship with the same group to which they may develop strong feelings of loyalty and duty. Most Japanese have a great respect for authority. They are very honest and tourists losing their bags will almost always get them back – and with any money still in them!

EDUCATION

The Japanese education system is good, but very competitive. Compulsory education starts at five, but there is so much competition to get into the best schools that

eight out of ten children go to kindergarten from the age of three. Elementary school lasts for six years and middle school for three years. These nine years of education are compulsory but most children go to high school for a further three years. One in three go on to university.

Homework is given from a very early age and many children spend their summers at private cramming schools so they will get into university.

RELIGION

The main religions are Shintoism and Buddhism. Most people combine beliefs and ceremonies from both in their daily lives. For example most Japanese have a Shinto wedding but prefer a Buddhist funeral.

The Shinto religion is found only in Japan. Shinto means 'way of the gods'. The Japanese recognise millions of gods called KAMI who live in natural places such as rivers, lakes and trees. These sites are sacred and each one has a shrine or temple. A gateway

◀ *Buddhism developed in India and came to Japan in the 6th century AD. Buddha means 'the enlightened one'. The Buddha was a living person who left his rich and powerful family to search for the meaning of life. After many years of poverty he achieved his aim. Buddhists try to follow his teachings so they too can find the meaning of life. The Japanese consider Shintoism is concerned with their daily life and that Buddhism prepares them for the after life.*

RELIGIOUS FESTIVALS AND HOLIDAYS

Festivals are associated with the rhythms of nature and religious beliefs.

1 January NEW YEAR'S DAY
A national holiday. Most businesses close from 1–3 January. It is the most important celebration of the year. Homes are decorated for a 'long, strong and prosperous year'. There are special foods, gifts and family visits.

15 January ADULTS' DAY
There are ceremonies for everyone over the age of 20.

11 February NATIONAL FOUNDATION DAY
A national holiday to celebrate when the first Japanese Emperor, Jimmu Tenno, came to the throne in 660 BC.

3 March GIRLS' DAY
Not an official holiday but widely observed. Girls go to each others' homes to admire collections of dolls which are lovingly made by craftspeople and passed on from one generation to the next.

20 or 21 March VERNAL EQUINOX DAY
A national holiday to celebrate the coming of spring. Visits are made to family graves.

29 April GREENERY DAY
The beginning of 'Golden Week' when most people take a whole week off work.

3 May CONSTITUTION DAY
A national holiday to commemorate the new constitution of 1947.

5 May CHILDREN'S DAY (formerly Boys' Day)
A national holiday. If there is a son in the family, a pole is erected in the garden with paper and cloth streamers shaped like carp attached. These are signs of energy, determination and ambition. There are also models of warriors.

In August O-BON FESTIVAL
A day for visiting shrines and dancing because it is the night when the souls of the departed return to Earth.

15 September RESPECT FOR THE AGED DAY

23 September AUTUMNAL EQUINOX DAY
A national holiday to celebrate the approach of autumn and a day for visiting the family graves.

10 October SPORTS DAY OR PHYSICAL CULTURE DAY
Introduced to commemorate the holding of the Olympics in Tokyo in 1964.

3 November CULTURE DAY
A national holiday to encourage people to enjoy peace and culture. It was the birthday of Mutsuhito (Meiji) who was emperor from 1867–1912.

23 November LABOUR THANKSGIVING DAY
A national holiday often combined with harvest festivals. The Emperor makes a ritual offering of SAKE to the gods.

23 December THE EMPEROR'S BIRTHDAY

31 December NEW YEAR'S EVE
Bells at important temples ring out 108 times at midnight to mark the end of the old year.

There are also many colourful regional and local festivals with processions and floats, singing, shouting and dancing. For example one is held in Kyoto during July to celebrate the founding of the city.

There are about 80,000 Shinto shrines and every community has at least one. Prayers are often pinned up by visitors. Before exams many students pin up prayers asking for good results.

or TORRII marks the entrance to the site. Visiting these sites is especially popular at annual festivals. Important historical figures, such as warriors, have also been regarded as gods. Until the end of the Second World War, the Emperor of Japan was worshipped as a god.

FAMILY LIFE

The average age of marriage is 28.3 years for men and 25.6 years for women. This is higher than in most industrial countries.

◀ Baseball has become very popular and Japan has the world's largest baseball leagues. The players are treated as stars, like top athletes all over the world.

Marriages used to be arranged by match makers, but today this is rare.

The average working week is 41.5 hours, also higher than in other industrial countries. Workers are also expected to go out with their colleagues after work. They will not get home until late so a father sees little of his family except on Sunday. Even if a job allows two weeks' holiday a year, most workers do not take it all.

LEISURE ACTIVITIES
Many popular leisure activities, such as SUMO, JUDO and KENDO, are part of Japanese culture. Others, such as golf and baseball, have been adopted from the West.

The most popular leisure activity is gardening. Even people living in flats have a window box and pot plants. Almost every house has a small plot 2 metres by 2 metres which may contain just a single tree, one or two large rocks and sand or gravel raked into patterns.

Japan also has a long tradition of different types of theatre including BUNRAKU, KABUKI and NOH.

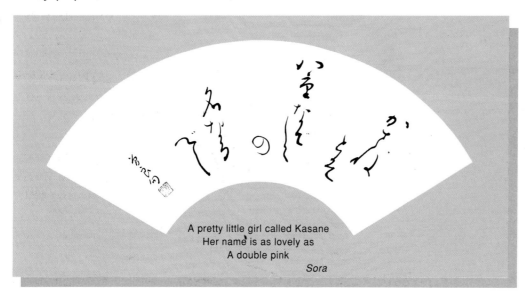

A pretty little girl called Kasane
Her name is as lovely as
A double pink
Sora

◀ A type of poem that is unique to Japan is the haiku. It usually consists of three short lines. This haiku was written by the poet Kawai Sora (1649–1710).

KEY FACTS

● 94% of children stay at school until the age of 18.

● Only 1 in 5 university students are women.

● 2 workers in 5 are women but their average pay is half that of men.

● Japan produced the world's first novel about AD 1000.

● Percentage of members of religions in Japan

Shinto	39.5
Buddhism	38.3
Christian	3.8
Others	18.4

▲ *Two girls wear the traditional* KIMONO *in a festival which celebrates reaching seven years of age. The* OBI *holds the gowns in place.*

◀ *Sumo wrestling is an ancient sport and is celebrated here at a festival. A wrestler or* RIKISHI *weighs over 130 kilos.*

RULE AND LAW

Japan has been a country since 200 BC. It has been ruled by emperors who, until 1946, were regarded as gods descended from Amaterasu the Sun goddess. However, for much of the time the emperors had little power. The country was controlled by the SHOGUN, the head of one of three powerful families. The shoguns controlled the warriors known as SAMURAI and ruled the country as they liked.

In 1867 the emperor Mutsuhito regained power from the shoguns and introduced a programme of reforms. He opened Japan to western ideas which the shoguns had excluded for over 200 years.

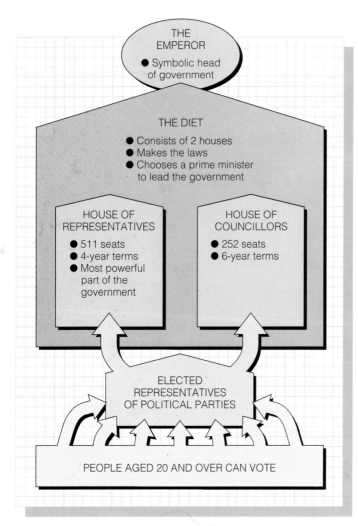

THE EMPEROR
● Symbolic head of government

THE DIET
● Consists of 2 houses
● Makes the laws
● Chooses a prime minister to lead the government

HOUSE OF REPRESENTATIVES
● 511 seats
● 4-year terms
● Most powerful part of the government

HOUSE OF COUNCILLORS
● 252 seats
● 6-year terms

ELECTED REPRESENTATIVES OF POLITICAL PARTIES

PEOPLE AGED 20 AND OVER CAN VOTE

▲ *Anyone over 20 can vote for politicians to represent them in the national government.*

▼ *Under the constitution introduced after the Second World War, Japan will not settle international conflicts by war.*

CHAPTER II. RENUNCIATION OF WAR

ARTICLE 9. Aspiring sincerely to an international peace based on justice and order, the Japanese people forever renounce war as a sovereign right of the nation and the threat or use of force as means of settling international disputes.

In order to accomplish the aim of the preceding paragraph, land, sea, and air forces, as well as other war potential, will never be maintained. The right of belligerency of the state will not be recognized.

Japan became stronger and occupied several countries in Asia, including Korea and parts of Russia and China. It fought against the Allies in the Second World War and finally surrendered when atomic bombs were dropped on Hiroshima and Nagasaki in 1945.

The USA occupied Japan from 1945 to 1952. A new constitution was drawn up. Hirohito (emperor from 1926 to 1989) remained the ruler, but he became a constitutional monarch like the king or queen of Britain. When he died in 1989, his son Akihito became emperor.

The country is divided into 47 prefectures with a governor and an assembly of elected people providing local government.

KEY FACTS

● Nippon (or Nihon) is the Japanese word for Japan. It means 'source of the Sun'.
● In 1945 the American general Douglas MacArthur ordered Emperor Hirohito to state publicly that he was not a god.
● There are few murders in Japan, only 1.4 a year for every 100,000 people. In the USA there are 8.7.

▼ *Japanese people are very law abiding and there is little robbery or violence. Community spirit is strong and the police are part of the community.*

FOOD AND FARMING

Farms are very small, usually only one or two hectares. A farmer may have three or four fields in different places around the village.

Rice is the most widely grown crop. The chief growing area used to be the warm island of Kyushu in the south where two crops a year can be grown. New varieties of rice can now be grown in the cooler climate of northern Honshu and this area has become more important than Kyushu. Other crops include tomatoes, aubergines, carrots, sweet potatoes, onions, water melons and strawberries.

The slopes above the PADDY FIELDS are terraced to make small level fields. Here farmers plant cereals such as wheat and barley or trees and bushes. Apples and pears are grown in the cooler north, while tea, mandarins, tangerines, peaches and nectarines are grown in the south.

Traditionally farmers have not kept animals for food but eating habits are changing and large numbers of poultry are now kept for their meat and eggs. In the south of Japan a farmer might keep a few beef cattle. The meat from these animals is very expensive because there is so little grazing that they have to be hand-reared.

◀ *Fish is eaten at most meals. Japan's fishing fleet is the world's biggest. It catches 12.7 million tonnes a year, about one-eighth of all fish caught in the world.*

KEY FACTS

● In Japan there is only 0.04 of a hectare of farmland for each person.
● Most cities now have western-style eating places like Macdonalds and Pizza Hut. Family meals are more traditional.
● Raw fish dishes such as SUSHI and

SASHIMI are very popular. So is the poisonous FUGU.
● Mulberry trees cover 90,000 hectares of land, mainly in central Honshu. The leaves feed silk worms which produce 40,000 tonnes of silk a year.

▲ *Rice is the main food and is eaten at almost every meal. It is grown on about half of all farmland. Farms and fields are small so large modern machinery cannot be used.*

▼ *The evening family meal is generally a traditional Japanese one eaten with chopsticks. Western-style diets are increasingly common.*

The meat is used in dishes such as SUKIYAKI.

Hokkaido is becoming an important agricultural area. Its cool, moist climate provides excellent pasture for dairy cattle and is suitable for the crops grown to supply western-style diets.

The Japanese eat three times as much fish as meat and fishing has always been important. The fishing fleets go to the Pacific, Indian and Atlantic oceans. Japanese farmers often breed fish in ponds and tanks on their farms. Now fish farms have also been set up just off the shore. Edible seaweed is also popular.

The Japanese still hunt whales for 'scientific purposes'. Whale meat is another popular delicacy but it can cost £140 a kilo.

▲ *Attractive presentation of food is important in Japanese cuisine. Lunch boxes are no exception!*

▶ *Japan produces 70 per cent of its food. Farms are tiny, so most farmers have another job.*

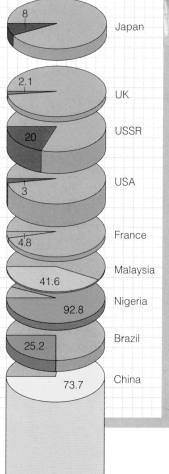

% OF WORKFORCE IN AGRICULTURE, 1990
(depth = no. in workforce)

8	Japan
2.1	UK
20	USSR
3	USA
4.8	France
41.6	Malaysia
92.8	Nigeria
25.2	Brazil
73.7	China

In just over 100 years Japan has changed from a poor farming country to a rich industrial one. Before 1868 there were only a few small factories making products

▲ This oil refinery in Tokyo Bay is built on land reclaimed from the sea. Japan imports crude oil and turns it into products such as petrol, diesel fuel and oil.

like silk, paper and pottery. The Emperor Mutsuhito, now usually known as Meiji, introduced western ideas and technology. He modernised agriculture, opened coal and copper mines, improved roads and built railways. From 1880 to the 1930s Japan produced its own textiles, steel, machinery and vehicles but few were exported.

The most spectacular industrial growth has taken place since 1950 and the main industries of Europe and America now face stiff competition from the Japanese. The first industry to suffer was ship-building, then motorcycles, cars and other vehicles, cameras, electrical goods, hi-fi equipment and musical instruments. In

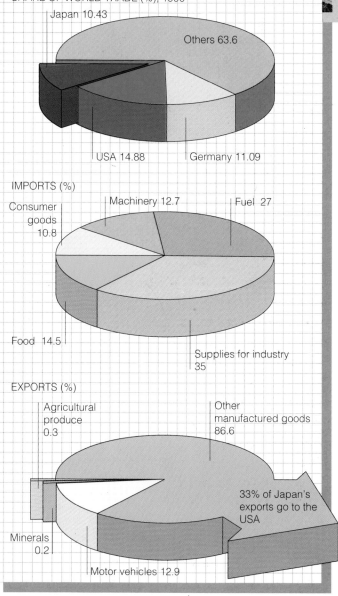

SHARE OF WORLD TRADE (%), 1990

Japan 10.43
Others 63.6
USA 14.88
Germany 11.09

IMPORTS (%)

Consumer goods 10.8
Machinery 12.7
Fuel 27
Food 14.5
Supplies for industry 35

EXPORTS (%)

Agricultural produce 0.3
Other manufactured goods 86.6
Minerals 0.2
33% of Japan's exports go to the USA
Motor vehicles 12.9

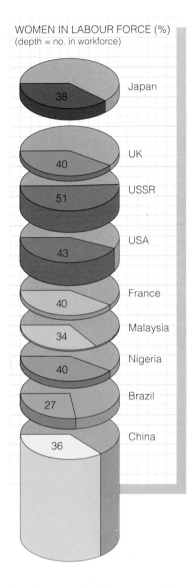

WOMEN IN LABOUR FORCE (%)
(depth = no. in workforce)

- Japan 38
- UK 40
- USSR 51
- USA 43
- France 40
- Malaysia 34
- Nigeria 40
- Brazil 27
- China 36

▶ *Japan is the world's biggest producer of electrical and electronic goods.*

fact Japan now makes most types of industrial goods. Japanese companies are successful because they invest large sums of money in developing new products, have good management and loyal employees, produce good value, high quality goods, have millions of customers in Japan and have been encouraged to sell their products abroad.

THE IRON AND STEEL INDUSTRY

The steel industry is the foundation of modern Japan. Steel is used in buildings, ships, vehicles and most consumer goods. Production has increased from 5 million tonnes a year in 1950 to around 106 million tonnes a year today.

Japan imports 99 per cent of its iron ore. Australia provides about 40 per cent, Brazil

► *Japanese companies are setting up factories in the countries where they sell many of their goods. This Nissan car factory at Sunderland in Britain has been so successful it is being expanded. Cars made here are sold in Britain and other European countries.*

25 per cent and India 20 per cent. The other raw material needed is coal and Japan has to import about 96 per cent of this. About 60 million tonnes are imported a year, 24 million from Australia, 16 million from Canada and 10 million from the USA. Around 30 million tonnes of steel are exported, mainly to China, Taiwan, South Korea and the USA.

The main steel-making plants have been built along the southern coast of Honshu, between Tokyo and Hiroshima. Some, like that at Oita on Kyushu, are built on land reclaimed from the sea.

THE SHIP-BUILDING INDUSTRY

Half the ships sailing today were built in Japan. In the 1960s and 1970s, huge shipyards made the ships Japan needed to take raw materials and manufactured goods to and from the rest of the world. These yards built the first oil supertankers.

The shipyards were built close to the steel works because steel is used to make ships. The industry has declined since its peak in the mid 1970s, but it still builds about 40 per cent of the world's shipping.

MOTOR INDUSTRY

The first Japanese-made cars arrived in Europe and the USA during the 1960s. At first, car manufacturers did not consider them serious competitors. Today, however, Japan has the largest motor industry of any country producing about 8.2 million cars and 7.6 million trucks and buses a year. About half of these are sold abroad, mainly to North America and Europe. Giant car-carrying ships capable of holding 6000 cars transport the cars to overseas markets.

The motor industry has been very successful. It employs around 5 million people in Japan alone. Mitsubishi, one of the biggest manufacturers, now builds vehicles in more than 30 countries and sells them in about 160.

ELECTRICAL GOODS

Japan decided to switch from heavy industries like iron and steel-making and ship-building

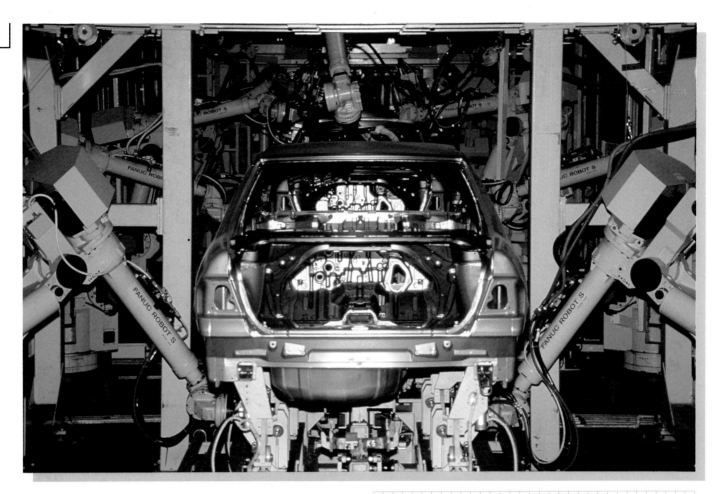

▲ *Robots do much of the building and painting in this Nissan car factory. They cost less than people and can work in unhealthy environments.*

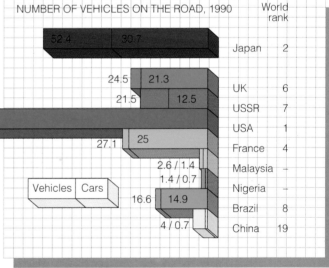

NUMBER OF VEHICLES ON THE ROAD, 1990	Vehicles	Cars		World rank
Japan	52.4	30.7		2
UK	24.5	21.3		6
USSR	21.5	12.5		7
USA	183.5	140.6		1
France	27.1	25		4
Malaysia	2.6	1.4		–
Nigeria	1.4	0.7		–
Brazil	16.6	14.9		8
China	4	0.7		19

KEY FACTS

● On a Honda assembly line, one car is completed every 43 seconds.

● There are factories in Japan where robots are making more robots.

● An employee of a big company expects to work for that company for life.

● Toyota City used to be called Koromo, but with 90% of the workforce employed by Toyota the name was changed.

● The world's 10 largest banks are all Japanese.

because they depended on imported raw materials and energy supplies. Instead, they developed industries like the electrical industry which needs a well educated workforce but few raw materials.

The output of electrical goods is immense. In 1990 Japan produced 352 million watches, 68 million calculators, 29 million stereo

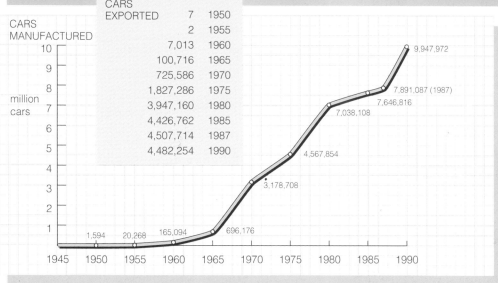

NUMBER OF CARS EXPORTED	Year
7	1950
2	1955
7,013	1960
100,716	1965
725,586	1970
1,827,286	1975
3,947,160	1980
4,426,762	1985
4,507,714	1987
4,482,254	1990

CARS MANUFACTURED

million cars

Graph values: 1,594 · 20,268 · 165,094 · 696,176 · 3,178,708 · 4,567,854 · 7,038,108 · 7,646,816 · 7,891,087 (1987) · 9,947,972

Years: 1945 1950 1955 1960 1965 1970 1975 1980 1985 1990

▲ *Japanese companies spend large sums of money developing new products. This car has a computer to help the driver avoid traffic jams. In the future all cars may have one, so earning the company a lot of money.*

recorders, 28 million video recorders, 13 million colour TVs, 6 million microwave ovens, 4 million fax machines, 2.5 million computers and 56,000 industrial robots.

These figures do not include all the electrical products put together in Japanese factories in neighbouring countries, such as Taiwan, Malaysia, South Korea and Hong Kong, where wages and other costs are lower. However the research into improving products and making new ones is still carried out in Japan. Japanese companies also find it profitable to establish factories in the countries where they sell most goods such as the UK or the USA.

◄ *Japanese companies are always searching for new products to make and export. Having started with electric organs and keyboards, Japan now produces high quality musical instruments including pianos, harps, violins and guitars. Japan is one of the biggest manufacturers of electrical goods in the world and a producer of world-class competition motor-bikes.*

WORKING FOR A JAPANESE COMPANY

Industry in Japan is dominated by a few large companies such as Toyota or Mitsubishi. When people go to work for them, they become part of a 'family' and expect to be cared for by the company for life. Companies often have whole suburbs or small cities for their employees to live in and accommodation is likely to be cheaper than finding it privately. Companies may provide scholarships for the children of employees, health care, annual parties and even annual holidays. In return, the companies expect loyalty and hard work.

In the factories there are no big divisions between the management and the factory workers. The views of people from all levels in the company are valued. There are no strikes.

▲ **The Stock Exchange in Tokyo is where companies and individuals can buy and sell shares in Japan's companies. Banking, insurance and other financial services employ more than two million people. The currency used in Japan is the yen.**

TRANSPORT

Although made up of islands, Japan has extremely efficient transport systems. Roads and railways are the main carriers. Ferry and air services link the smaller islands.

Like large cities in all developed countries, the roads are clogged with vehicles, especially at rush-hours. Most people use the local trains or underground in the major cities like Tokyo. They are among the most efficient and overcrowded in the world.

An excellent rail network links the major cities. Besides the government-owned Japanese Railways, there are also private railway companies. Japan pioneered high-speed trains in the 1960s and today there are three high-speed lines, which all start from Tokyo. The first line was built to the west. It links Tokyo with other industrial centres, such as Nagoya and Osaka, and terminates at Fukoka on Kyushu.

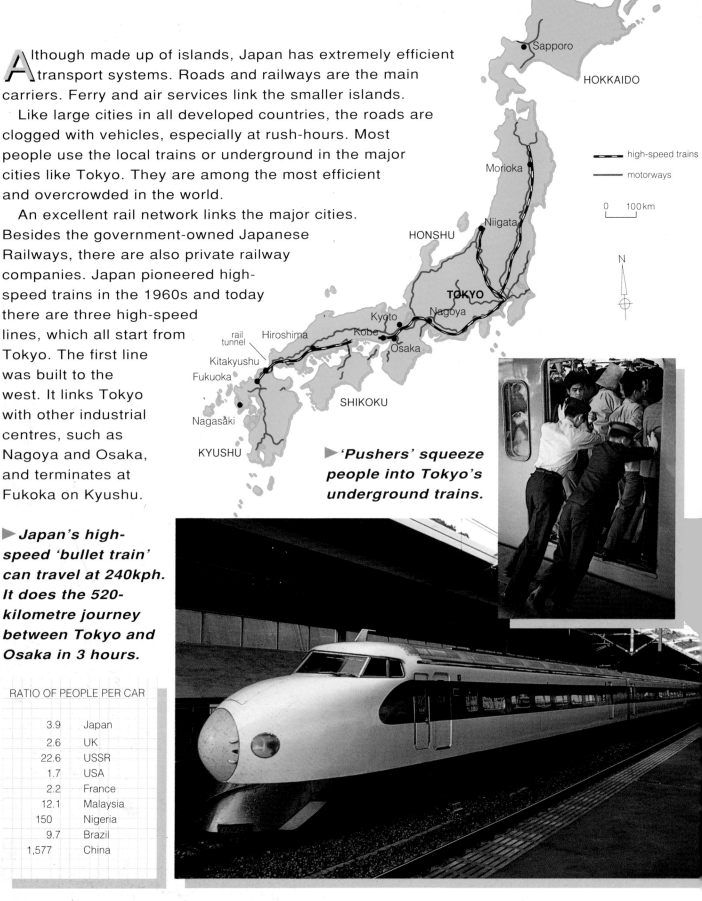

HOKKAIDO
Sapporo

HONSHU
Morioka
Niigata
TOKYO
Nagoya
Kyoto
Kobe
Osaka
Hiroshima
rail tunnel
Kitakyushu
Fukuoka
Nagasaki
SHIKOKU
KYUSHU

- - - high-speed trains
——— motorways

0   100km

N

► *'Pushers' squeeze people into Tokyo's underground trains.*

► *Japan's high-speed 'bullet train' can travel at 240kph. It does the 520-kilometre journey between Tokyo and Osaka in 3 hours.*

RATIO OF PEOPLE PER CAR	
3.9	Japan
2.6	UK
22.6	USSR
1.7	USA
2.2	France
12.1	Malaysia
150	Nigeria
9.7	Brazil
1,577	China

Another line runs north across the country to Niigata and a third north-east to Morioka in the north of Honshu.

The road system is being improved constantly to cope with the 30.7 million cars and 21.4 million lorries that use it. Motorways now link all the major cities. Roads carry 93 per cent of all freight.

Tunnels and bridges join the four major islands. The Seikan Tunnel between Honshu and Hokkaido is 43 kilometres long and is the longest underwater rail tunnel until the Channel Tunnel between France and the UK opens in 1993. The longest suspension bridge in the world is being built in Japan. The Akashi Kaikyo Road Bridge is due for completion in 1998. Its overall span will measure 1,990 metres across and it will link the islands of Honshu and Shikoku.

▲ *Huge bridges have been built to speed up travel between Japan's islands. The Seto Ohashi bridge links several of the smaller islands.*

KEY FACTS

● The Japanese drive on the left of the road.
● There are 27,454 kilometres of railways and 1.1 million kilometres of roads.
● The railways carry almost 21 million inter-city passengers a year and 83 million tonnes of freight.
● Japan is the only country in the world which uses jumbo jets for internal passenger flights due to the high number of people wishing to travel.

Japan has become a very wealthy country because its industries have been extremely successful. Until recently few people, in Japan or any other industrialised country, realised it was important to protect the environment. People and the environment suffered as a result. Now Japan has some of the strictest anti-pollution laws in the world.

In and around the cities the air is badly polluted by the fumes from factories and vehicles. Doctors now recognise diseases caused by pollution, such as Yokkaichi asthma suffered by people living near the Yokkaichi chemical works at Kawasaki.

Many rivers in the industrial areas are so badly polluted by factories that they can no longer be used to supply drinking water. In

▲ *Away from the cities much of the country is wild and beautiful. National parks, like this one at Takao near Kyoto, have been set up in all parts of Japan to protect the countryside from development.*

▼ *Sulphur dioxide and nitrogen oxides are the main causes of acid rain.*

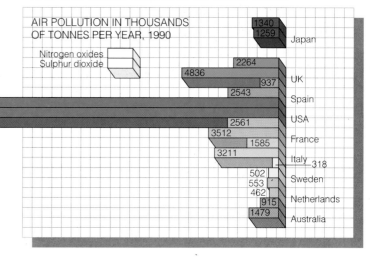

AIR POLLUTION IN THOUSANDS OF TONNES PER YEAR, 1990

Nitrogen oxides
Sulphur dioxide

Country	Nitrogen oxides	Sulphur dioxide
Japan	1340	1259
UK	2264	937
Spain	2543	4836
USA	20300	23900
France	2561	1585
Italy	3512	3211
Sweden	502	318
Netherlands	553	462
Australia	915	1479

1971 people living near the Toruku mine on Kyushu became very ill because their water had been poisoned with arsenic used at the mine. People are still suffering and dying from its effects.

The polluted water from industry and the cities ends up in the sea. Seafood such as oysters and fish caught in these waters can be dangerous to eat. One of the worst pollution disasters ever was at Minamata on Kyushu. Mercury from a chemical works was allowed to run into the sea where it was taken in by sea creatures. When these were eaten, the poison went into people. Affected people could not see, hear or speak properly and lost their sense of touch. Over 750 have died since 1953 when the disease, now known as Minamata disease, was first recognised.

KEY FACTS

● Japan has 50 million tonnes of waste to dispose of a year.
● Much is put in the sea to make new land.
● The Kawasaki milk carton recycling group collects old milk cartons to turn into toilet paper.
● In major cities 30% of drinking water wells are contaminated with chemicals and unfit for drinking.

▲ *Japan is one of the few countries that still hunts whales. In 1991 the whaling fleet set out to catch 330 minke whales in the Antarctic. Commercial whaling is banned, but the whales are killed, so it is said, to allow scientists to learn more about them.*

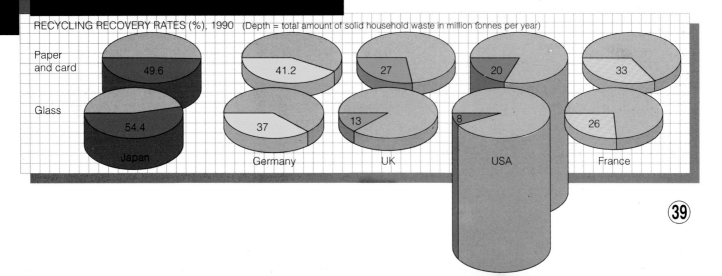

RECYCLING RECOVERY RATES (%), 1990 (Depth = total amount of solid household waste in million tonnes per year)

	Japan	Germany	UK	USA	France
Paper and card	49.6	41.2	27	20	33
Glass	54.4	37	13	8	26

◀Half of Japan's population lives along the Kanto Plain. The towns spread over huge areas and getting from one place to another creates terrible congestion and air pollution. This is a motorway out of Tokyo at the height of the evening rush-hour, though from the size of the jam, 'rush' is not the right word!

Japan is criticised by international environmental groups like Greenpeace and the World Wide Fund for Nature for failing to protect the environment. People were shocked by pictures from the island of Fukue of fishermen clubbing more than 500 dolphins to death, supposedly to protect their fish.

However, pressure for environmental protection is growing rapidly. People living on the Shiraho coral reef off the island of Ishigaki fought for 11 years to prevent a new airport being built on the reef and destroying its unique wildlife. The airport will still be built but on another coral reef where it will do less harm.

Air pollution is becoming less as more laws come into force. Factories have to clean their smoke before it goes into the air. As a result, the air in some cities contains only one-sixth of the sulphur dioxide it did in the 1960s. All new cars are fitted with catalytic converters which reduce pollution from car exhausts. Japan is also trying to save resources by recycling paper and glass.

THE FUTURE

Japan has come a long way since the end of the Second World War. Then, to help the country recover, Japanese industries were protected from imported foreign goods. This is still the case. No-one then imagined that before the end of the century Japan would be the world's leading industrial nation. In fact, when Japanese goods started to arrive in western countries in the 1960s, they were described as cheap, tinny and shoddy. People never dreamed that within 30 years they would be trying to copy Japan's economic example. Today, Japan makes two-thirds of all computer chips and electronic consumer goods. Its economic power dominates the world. It owns more businesses and property in overseas countries than any other country, including the USA, it has the world's leading stock exchange and the largest trade surplus ever known.

A country has a trade surplus when it earns more money from what it sells overseas than what it spends on buying things from overseas. Each year Japan exports goods worth US $275,000 million and imports goods worth US $210,000 million, giving it a very large trade surplus indeed. Some of the main importing countries, such as the USA and Britain, complain that the Japanese are unfair and make it difficult for countries trying to sell goods in Japan, while Japanese goods can enter other countries without difficulty. As a result, many countries now limit the number of Japanese goods they import.

Another complaint is that Japanese goods are cheaper than similar ones made in the West because the goods are not made in Japan but in the neighbouring countries where the companies can pay lower wages than in Japan or the West.

Japanese companies are also criticised for showing little respect for the peoples or environments of the countries from which they import resources like coal and timber.

◄ *Japan uses advanced forms of computer graphics to illustrate new ideas in design and technology. Here is a representation of a new building that will be constructed using robots.*

◀ *These teenagers are among many who are trying to break away from the strict traditions of their parents. The music and clothing styles of the West have a strong influence on Japanese youth today.*

Another criticism is that Japan is a wealthy country but takes little part in international events, such as the Gulf War, or peace-keeping in other countries. However, Japan does give more aid to developing countries than any other country.

The Japanese have been hurt by these criticisms and there are signs that they are changing their policies.

Apart from their relationship with other countries, the Japanese face a serious problem at home: overcrowding and lack of space. Japanese architects and engineers have proposed some fantastic solutions. One is to build cities stretching high into the sky.

Japan is not the only country with the problem of overcrowding. Plans were made to host a world conference and exhibition in 1994 that would look at living in cities in the 21st century. An estimated twenty million visitors were expected.

The economic and industrial success of Japan since the destruction of the Second World War has been phenomenal. Although there are hints that some young people in Japan are beginning to question their highly organised, highly competitive way of life, it will be a very long time before Japan loses its economic supremacy.

KEY FACTS

● The population balance will change by the year 2000. In 1980 9% of the population was aged 65 or over. In 2000 this figure will be 15.6%.

● It is expected that by the year 2000 the number of old people receiving pensions will be about four times more than in 1980.

● Japan will continue in the 1990s with research and development 'offshore' (not within Japan). In 1991–92 over 12 companies opened laboratories in Britain encouraging foreign researchers to develop ideas and build new products.

▲ *Young designers are encouraged to create fantastic vehicles at the Toyota Idea Expo. The "Neo Cosmic Voyager"* *shown here can hug the ground like a sportscar or raise itself up to move over obstacles.*

FURTHER INFORMATION

JAPAN AIRLINES, 5 Hanover Square, London W1R 0DR.
Selection of posters, booklets and leaflets.
JAPAN INFORMATION AND CULTURAL CENTRE, Japanese Embassy, 101–104 Piccadilly, London W1V 0AH.
Produces a wide range of teaching resources.
JAPAN NATIONAL TOURIST ORGANISATION, 167 Regent Street, London W1R 7FD.
JAPAN TRAVEL BUREAU, 190 The Strand, London WC2R 1DT.

BOOKS ABOUT JAPAN
A family in Japan, Jacobsen and Kristensen, Wayland 1984 (age 9–14)
Focus on Japan, Mavis Pilbeam, Hamish Hamilton 1987 (age 8–16)
A Geography of Japan, Donald MacDonald, Paul Norbury 1985 (age 13–18)

Great Civilisations – Japan 5000 BC to Today, Mavis Pilbeam, Franklin Watts 1988 (age 8–14)
Japanese Fairy Book, Yei Theodora Ozaki, Tuttle 1970 (age 11 upward)
Japanese Family, Judith Elkin, A&C Black 1986 (age 11–14)
Japanese Food and Drink, Lesley Downer, Wayland 1987 (age 9 upward)
Let's go to Japan, Gwyneth Ashby, Franklin Watts 1985 (age 8–12)
Origami in Colour, Zulal Aytura–Scheel, Octopus Books 1986 (age 12 upward)
Passport to Japan, Richard Tames, Franklin Watts 1988 (age 8–12)
Places and Peoples in the World: Japan, Rebecca Stefoff, Chelsea House 1988 (age 13 upward)
A Samurai Warrior, Anne Steel, Wayland 1986 (age 9–16)

● GLOSSARY

BUNRAKU
Stage plays acted by puppets accompanied by a story-teller and musician.

FUGU
Fugu is made from a poisonous blowfish.

JUDO
A form of wrestling. Two contestants take part on a mat 9 metres square. They score points by achieving various locks, holds or throws against their opponent.

KABUKI
Plays written from the 17th century onwards about ancient legends of love and war. All the women's roles are played by men.

KAMI
The Shinto spirits which live in sacred places on Earth such as rivers and lakes.

KENDO
Coming from samurai sword fighting, contestants use bamboo staffs or wooden swords to try to strike precise target areas on each others' bodies.

KIMONO
The traditional dress of Japanese men and women dating from the 7th century. The ankle-length dress is normally silk, and has long broad sleeves. It wraps over in front and is tied with an obi. Now mainly worn by women on special occasions.

NOH
Plays about the old-fashioned life of Japanese aristocrats. The actors wear elaborate masks.

OBI
The wide waist sash used to tie a kimono.

PADDY FIELDS
Fields in which rice is grown. Rice is a marsh plant and the fields are surrounded with low banks and flooded.

RIKISHI
A sumo wrestler. He can weigh over 130 kilogrammes but is very agile.

SAKE
An alcoholic drink made from rice. It is often drunk warm.

SAMURAI
The soldiers who formed a ruling class in Japan until the 19th century.

SASHIMI
A dish of pieces of raw fish.

SHOGUN
Military rulers who controlled the Emperor and ruled Japan for nearly 700 years.

SUKIYAKI
A meal made with thin strips of beef, vegetables and seasoning. It is usually cooked at the table and eaten immediately.

SUMO
A form of wrestling. Two rikishi in a circular ring each try to make his opponent step outside the ring or touch the ground with part of his body other than the feet.

SUSHI
A special meal of cold rice and raw fish.

TORRII
The elaborate gateways close to many Shinto shrines.

YEN
The currency used in Japan. One yen is divided into 100 sen – a unit seldom used today.

INDEX

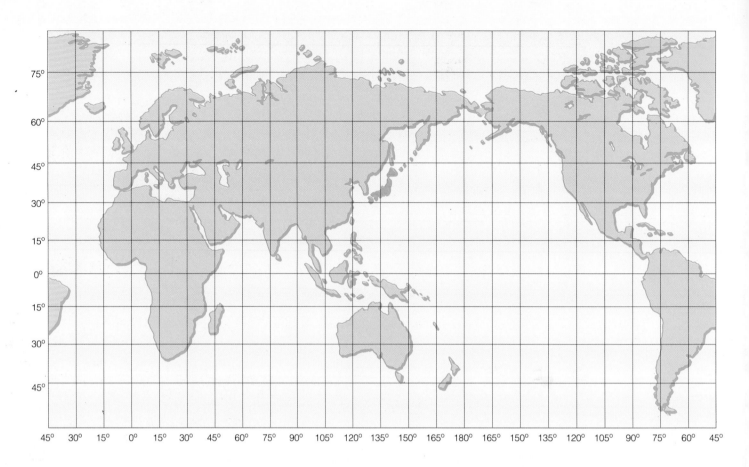

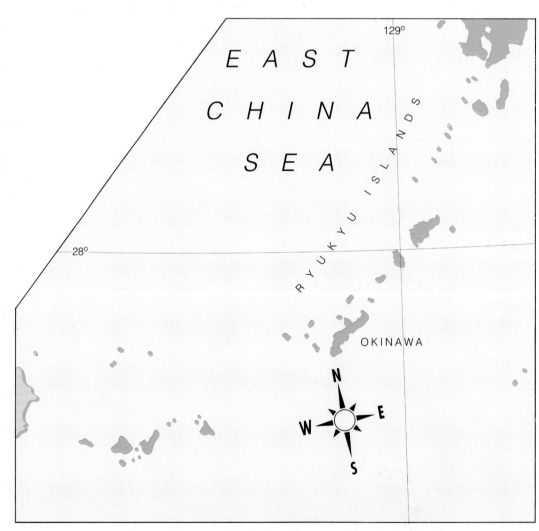

EAST
CHINA
SEA

RYUKYU ISLANDS

OKINAWA

129°

28°

N
W E
S

135°

CIS

HOKKAIDO

Kushiro

Otaru • Sapporo

S E A

O F

J A P A N

Aomori

40°

Akita • Morioka

Sendai

H O N S H U

Niigata

Hitachi

TOKYO

Fukui

Chiba

Kawasaki

Yokohama

Lake Biwa

Matsue

Kyoto • Nagoya

Kobe

Okayama • Osaka

Hiroshima

SEA

INLAND

Tokushima

KOREA STRAIT

TSU
ISLANDS

Kitakyushu

Kochi

Fukuoka

SHIKOKU

JAPAN

Kumamoto

Nagasaki

Kagoshima

KYUSHU

RYUKYU

ISLANDS

0   100km

P A C I F I C   O C E A N

INA

RTH
REA

UTH
REA